# The Power of Prayer

## of Prayer

*Plugging*
*into*
*the*
*source*

PRESENTED BY

*Jill Briscoe*

NexGen™ is an imprint of
Cook Communications Ministries, Colorado Springs, Colorado 80918
Cook Communications, Paris, Ontario
Kingsway Communications, Eastbourne, England

THE POWER OF PRAYER
© 2003 by *Just Between Us* magazine

First Printing, 2003
Printed in the United States of America

1 2 3 4 5 6 7 8 9 10 Printing/Year 07 06 05 04 03

This book is part of a series on relevant issues for today's Christian
woman. For more information on other titles in this series or for
information about *Just Between Us* magazine, please turn to the back of
this book.

 Library of Congress Cataloging-in-Publication Data
The power of prayer : plugging into the power source / [edited by] Jill
Briscoe.
     p. cm. -- (Just between us)
  ISBN 0-7814-3953-1 (booklet : pbk.)
  1.  Prayer--Christianity. 2.  Christian women--Religious life.  I. Briscoe,
Jill. II. Series.
  BV210.3.P69 2003
  248.3'2--dc21

                                              2003006901

# contents

A Note from Jill Briscoe . . . . . . . . . . . . . . . . . . . . . . . . *iv*
*Jill Briscoe*

**1** Prayer That Works . . . . . . . . . . . . . . . . . . . . . . . . . . . . . *1*
*Jill Briscoe*

**2** Praying When Life Gets Hard . . . . . . . . . . . . . . . . . . . . *12*
*Nancy J. Nordenson*

**3** Why Won't I Pray with My Wife? . . . . . . . . . . . . . . . . *20*
*Louis McBurney. M.D.*

**4** Praying Below the Surface . . . . . . . . . . . . . . . . . . . . . . . *27*
*Pamela Binkley*

**5** Praying for Your Husband . . . . . . . . . . . . . . . . . . . . . . . *33*
*Bette Morgan*

**6** Leading on Your Knees . . . . . . . . . . . . . . . . . . . . . . . . . *38*
*Shelly Esser*

**7** What's My Story? . . . . . . . . . . . . . . . . . . . . . . . . . . . . . *47*
*Lydia E. Harris*

**8** Digging Deeper: Prayer That Works . . . . . . . . . . . . . . . *50*
*Elizabeth Greene*

**9** Counseling Corner: The Female Cardinal Syndrome . . . . *54*
*Ingrid Lawrenz, MSW*

**10** How to Turn Your Prayer Meetings
into Blessings . . . . . . . . . . . . . . . . . . . . . . . . . . . . . . . . *58*
*Jill Briscoe*

# A Note from Jill Briscoe

Dear Friends,

One paraphrase of 1 Peter 5:7 says, "You can throw the whole weight of your anxieties upon Him for you are His personal concern."

Prayer and worry cannot live together. You cannot worry and pray at the same time. Prayer is the place to let your anxieties go—to hand them off to someone else, someone well able to carry them for you. God!

It's hard to throw the whole weight of our anxiety upon Him isn't it? How do we do that?

When I'm traveling, which seems to be constantly, I carry a briefcase full of files and books with me. It's heavy. When I'm on the road alone my back hurts by the end of the day. Often I'm with my husband, Stuart, or daughter, Judy, who hurry to take my briefcase to lift the load. I want to help so it's not an extra burden for them. Sometimes I say, "Let's both carry it. Let's share it." But the handle isn't big enough and it doesn't work. I've even been tempted to open the bag and take out some of the books to carry myself so it's lighter for them! But their backs are strong and well able to carry the case while my back is hurting, unable to carry it. So I *throw* my burden gratefully into their hands! They always smile at me because they love me and are concerned.

Occasionally I refuse their kind offer of help. Why? For all sorts of reasons. I get to thinking they have their own burdens, and I should be able to carry a little briefcase filled with a few books. Or I begin to worry that they'll dread having me along because I'm such a nuisance with my moving library! I always reap the consequences of carrying the stuff myself, when guilt, self-effort, pride, or stupidity lead me to refuse their helping hand.

I'm sure Stuart and Judy consider me very foolish when they are walking right beside me and are willing and able to help, but I insist on *going it alone*. I think God thinks we are very foolish too when He has told us to hand off our heavy issues to Him and we don't. So don't forget. God is your constant travel companion along life's road. His back is big enough and strong enough for your *case load* of worries. And don't be opening the bag and keeping a few books to carry yourself to make it easier on Him. Throw the whole weight of your anxieties upon Him for you are His personal concern.

In His Love,

*Jill Briscoe*

# chapter one

# *Prayer* That Works

### *Jill Briscoe*

*E*ver since I was a little girl in war-torn England, sitting on a three-legged stool in front of my house waiting for the bombs to fall, I have wanted my prayers to work. I remember praying, "Oh, God, please stop the war." He didn't, and I remember feeling very disappointed with Him. Maybe you have prayed that God would stop the conflict raging around you or in your own life, and He hasn't, and you feel disappointed with Him too. Maybe you feel like your prayers didn't work.

You may wonder what the words *prayer* and *work* are doing in the same sentence. Surely that sounds like an oxymoron! Do you know what an oxymoron is? It's when you put two seemingly contradictory words together, like jumbo shrimp, civil war, or child safe! Prayer and work seem to be opposite concepts. Yet I have discovered that prayer that doesn't work, doesn't work! It takes work to step out of time into eternity, and work to learn the art of leaving things undone so that the greater thing can be done.

Prayer that works isn't merely a matter of personality or gifting, though some people have a propensity for praying or have the gift of prayer (and this gift is something that worries the devil very much). Prayer itself is a gracious gift of God in the sense that He made it possible for us to walk right into His presence and talk to Him as our Father. Every child of God has that right and privilege.

But if Satan has his way, the first thing to go in our devotional life will be our devotional life! As the little couplet says, "The devil trembles when he sees the weakest saint upon his knees." He will do anything to stop us praying. Sometimes he doesn't have to do anything at all, however, because we assist him by doing away with our prayer life all on our own.

## When God Doesn't Seem to Answer

Often, one of the reasons we stop praying is that we're disappointed with the whole concept of prayer. When we urgently request something from God and He doesn't come through for us, we feel hurt and even betrayed that our prayers have not been answered. That's what happened to me when I was small.

I remember that first urgent attempt to call on the Almighty. The need arose when I became aware that someone was trying to kill me! The Second World War was in full swing, and I had the misfortune to live in Liverpool, a dangerous place. Ships supplying us with food from our allies brought their precious cargo to this seaport, making it a target for the enemy. I was very young, but I was aware that there was a God in heaven, and somewhere deep down in my heart I knew He was perfectly capable of stopping wars and conflicts. I decided one day that I would ask Him to stop these terrible airplanes from dropping bombs all over my life.

That night the air raids were particularly vicious. While we were huddled in our underground shelter like little moles, I confidently asked God to intervene. The answer came immediately: the bomb dropped far too near for comfort, damaging the back of our house and sending us running for shelter. *What went wrong?* I asked myself furiously, trying in my six-year-old mind to make sense out this nonsense. Had God not heard? Had I said my prayer with the wrong words or in the wrong way? Then came the unwelcome thought: *Perhaps God didn't hear me because He was too busy doing other things like keeping the stars in place.* And last came the worst thought: *Maybe He couldn't help me because He couldn't help me. He wasn't big enough or strong enough.*

Well, one way or another my fervent request had been ignored, and a huge sense of betrayal gripped me. Somewhere deep down in my six-year-old heart I determined not to try again. Not a few adults have faced similar dilemmas. At the first disappointment they quit without finding out what is happening and what makes prayer work.

If this is the case, the first thing we should do is pray about this. In fact, we should pray about anything that hinders our prayer life. You might want to stop this moment and ask the Lord to identify whatever has caused you to stop talking to Him. Then, when you have an inkling of what the blockage has been, talk to Him about it.

## Master the Art of Leaving Things Undone

The first thing you need to learn as you begin to pray prayers that work is to master the art of leaving things undone. Many of us suffer from "Martha syndrome." Martha was a woman who loved Jesus very much, but her "much serving" distracted her from focusing on Him (Luke 10:40, NKJV). It's hard to leave the urgent thing to attend to one's soul, but the Lord calls us to just such a duty. You have to learn to do it in the middle of the muddle! Martha had good reasons not to sit at Jesus' feet, but those reasons were not enough for the Lord. He said to her, "Martha, Martha! You are worried and upset about so many things, but only one thing is necessary. Mary has chosen what is best, and it will not be taken away from her" (Luke 10:41-42, NKJV). Many of us can get so excited about the work of the Lord that we forget the Lord of the work, as someone has so aptly said.

## Simply Get Started

But where do we start when we meet with God? One of the reasons some people avoid personal devotions is a fear of incompetence. *Whatever shall we say when we enter His throne room?* they wonder. Maybe we've always had a problem talking to important people. How do you address the King of kings and Lord of lords? The first thing to do is find a place and time for such an important conversation. Prayer must be planned. There is a sense in which prayer can be engaged in all day long. But time must also be put aside in order to visit with the King, and so plans should be made.

May I suggest that you take your calendar at the start of the week and pencil in time with the Lord every day. To see that appointment there in black and white sometimes helps you to keep it.

Finding a place can be more of a challenge. When I had young children, it was almost impossible to find a quiet spot. In desperation one day, I took the kids out of their playpen and climbed inside! This became a lifesaver for me, and in the busy days after I'd discovered this safe haven, the children learned to leave me alone. They decided that Mommy was a whole lot nicer when she got out than when she got in!

> **Life Lifters**
>
> "*P*rayer is the sweat of the soul."
>
> —**Martin Luther**—

## Learn to Be Still

But I still haven't addressed the problem of what to do when you actually get everything in order and are ready to pray. For instance, what do you do about wandering thoughts?

Let me give you an illustration. We have a cute grandchild, Stephen, who learned at an early age to avoid his mother's eyes when she wanted to talk to him. This necessitated his mom catching up with him and capturing him in her arms. She then turned him around and, taking his little face in a firm grip, got down on his level. Then she said gently, "Look at me, Stephen!" Stephen's eyes rolled to the left, then to the right, then right up to the top of his head until only the whites could be seen! Judy kept at it, holding his little face until, slightly dizzy with all that eye rolling, Stephen finally focused his eyes on his mother's face, and then she could tell him what she wanted him to hear. The first thing she said was, "I love you, Stephen." Then she told him what she needed to tell him.

When you begin to pray, imagine that you are Stephen! Think about God, your heavenly Father, taking your face lovingly in His hands and holding you firmly right there in front of Him saying to you, "Look at me, Stephen." Stay still until you focus. In other words, be still and know that He is God (Ps. 46:10). When your thoughts are settled, it's a good idea to start every time in God's presence with a period of silent prayer.

Try to form a habit of meeting with God without an agenda. So many of us have to teach or care for others that it is hard to come to God without thinking about them. Oh, we think, this Scripture would be excellent for Mrs. Smith. But God has things to say to us as well as to Mrs. Smith. We need to listen to God's voice without thinking of others and what would be good for them. First, God wants to tell us what is good for us. Listening to God is an important part of prayer. Try settling down to spend time quietly. Before you even begin to get down to the work of prayer, see if you can hear a thought, enjoy the stillness, or receive a new idea God wants you to think about.

In prayer, you have passive parts and active parts. Yet even the passive parts take work for some of us! It takes a huge effort to stop and be still, especially if we are active by nature. In the book of Hebrews, for example, the Lord says, "Make every effort to enter that rest" (Heb. 4:11). Here Paul puts two words together that do not appear to belong together at all, *effort* and *rest*. That sounds like another oxymoron. I am a very active person. It takes a big effort on my part to be quiet and still, but I must work at resting if I am to have any power in my prayer life. It is only after quieting our spirit that we will know what to pray and how to pray.

## Look at Those Who Pray Well

There are many ways of learning about prayer. One way is to look at the lives of people who seem to have gotten a handle on it. Who prays prayers that work?

It is said that James, the brother of our Lord Jesus Christ, had a nickname that was given to Him by the early church. He was called "camel knees"! The obvious inference is that James's knees resembled those of a camel because he was always kneeling. Hearing this caused me to wonder what my nickname might be!

We're going to take a close look at a prophet named Elijah. James pointed out, "Elijah was a man just like us. He prayed earnestly that it would not rain, and it did not rain on the land for three and a half years. Again he prayed, and the heavens gave rain, and the earth produced its crops" (James 5:17-18). Now there is a prayer that worked!

What sort of person do you need to be in order to be effective in your prayer life?

*You Have to Learn to Be Passionate*
*in Your Praying.*

Elijah "prayed earnestly that it would not rain, and it did not rain," (James 5:17). Elijah's heart was in his work. Many times we kneel to pray and we really don't care if God hears and answers us or not. Fervency is a condition of the heart that is developed through our growing relationship with God. As we grow to love Him, we find ourselves caring about the things He cares about. Prayer turns our thoughts away from our selfish concerns because we are putting ourselves into the presence of a selfless Being—and a little of that rubs off.

*You Need to Be a Persistent Pray-er if You Are to See Your Prayers Work.*

Elijah prayed continually about the work of God. He climbed a mountain and got to work. He set himself to watch and pray until the rain came (1 Kings 18:42-46). Most of us give up far too soon when we are praying. We hit an obstacle such as unanswered prayer and stop dead in our tracks. When Elijah set himself to pray on the top of Mount Carmel, you get the impression that he settled down until the answer came. God likes us to be persistent. Jesus told a story about a woman who persistently asked a judge to grant her request (see Luke 18:1-8). And Jesus commended the persistent, blind beggar (see Luke 18:35-43). He wants us to go on asking until it's the right time to get an answer. Persistence takes your prayer life into a whole new orbit. "Are any among you suffering? They should keep on praying about it" James tells us (James 5:13, NLT).

> ### LifeLifters
> "*P*rayer is the vital breath of the Christian; not the thing that makes him alive, but the evidence that he is alive."
> —**Oswald Chambers**—

## Pray When Trouble Troubles You

There should be no excuse for any of us. It's not

as if we have nothing to pray about! God has allowed enough trouble in all of our lives to keep us on our knees. And yet for some this could be the sticking point. It's hard to pray when trouble troubles us. Yet James sets his remarks about prayer in the context of trouble. "Is any one of you in trouble? He should pray" he says (James 5:13). We should, but do we? It has been my experience that my prayer life seizes up as soon as trouble pokes its ugly head into my life. But in the end I look back and recognize that without the trouble there would have been very little praying at all. If we are desperate enough, trouble forces us to spend time with God.

When we first came to live in America, our children were thrilled with the music programs in the public schools. All of them wanted to play an instrument. "I want to play the drums," seven-year-old Pete announced. I was aghast and hastily signed him up for clarinet. This was a serious mistake. The net result of all this was that he never practiced because he didn't want to play the clarinet; he wanted to play the drums. One day he came whistling into the room carrying his clarinet. "Pray for me, Mom," he said. "It's tryouts at school for band, and I want first chair clarinet!"

"I can't pray that for you, Pete. You haven't practiced in months."

"If I'd practiced, I wouldn't need you to pray," he retorted! Many of us are like Pete. We never practice prayer, but when urgent business arises, we expect to know exactly what to say and how to say it. Trouble gives us the grand opportunity to practice for the concert.

What sort of trouble was James talking about? All sorts. Little troubles and big ones. He mentions relational troubles: "Confess your sins to each other" (James 5:16). And he deals with sin troubles: "Whoever turns a sinner from the error of his way will save him from death and cover over a multitude of sins" (v. 20). Is any among you hurting? Has your spouse left you? Has someone mistreated you at work? Have you been passed over or gotten the bad part of a deal? Is there someone out there friendless, loveless, childless, cashless, jobless, powerless, clueless? "Is anyone in trouble? He should pray!"

Trouble is a great growth hormone. It takes us from being spiritual dwarfs to spiritual giants—if we respond rightly to it, that is. A few years ago, our family moved into crisis mode. I listened to myself praying. I was shocked. I heard myself like an unbeliever. I was praying panic prayers, indulging in angry tirades, and using bargaining language. "Where is my prayer life just when I need it the most?" I asked God. Hard on the heels of that thought came the realization that this trouble was going to do wonders for my prayer life! And it has. Trouble can, in fact, jump-start our prayer life. If we respond to divinely permitted trouble instead of reacting against it, we will find that the situation does two things for us. It will show us that our devotional life isn't working, and it will show us how to work on making it work!

God is such a God of grace. Sometimes He must feel very like the father whose son was in college and who only got in touch when he wanted money! Does the Lord hear from you and me only when we want something? The amazing thing about the Lord is His patient love. He will hear us out whenever we get around to approaching Him.

So when trouble comes, don't resist it as if it is an enemy; rather, welcome it as a friend. Let it drive you to your knees. Think about it. If trials persist, it just may be that you will persist in prayer. Looking back, I can see how constant pressure kept me in the Lord's presence, and for that I am grateful.

Never be afraid to ask God for the stars, but when God says no or wait, be willing to say, "Thy will be done," and ask the Lord for strength to live well in difficult circumstances. As we try to discover the secrets of prayer that works, it is my prayer that we will find our prayer lives revolutionized.

# chapter two

# *Praying*
# When Life Gets Hard

### How can you talk to God when your heart is breaking?

*Nancy J. Nordenson*

*I*n a dimly lit hospital room, I stared out the window into the early morning darkness and waited for the drips of IV fluid to begin the contractions that would birth my lifeless midterm baby. My sorrow was lonely and deep. I wanted to pray, but there were no words to voice the thoughts that swirled in my mind.

When life is hard, prayer is hard. Grief, illness, depression, and anger invade our lives and hang on with tenacity, stealing our desire to pray and our belief in prayer just when we need them most. Physically and emotionally weary, we struggle to move from "Dear God" to "Amen." Simply getting through the day becomes our goal, leaving the luxury of connecting with God for better times.

I find it difficult to meet the expectations of Scripture regarding prayer. I fail to pray "with thanksgiving" (Phil. 4:6) when the situation I've prayed about for so long is only getting worse. How many of us pray "without ceasing" (1 Thess. 5:17, KJV) when waves of grief knock us over, pull us down, and hold us under? When disappointment and anger over dashed plans and failed relationships consume our thoughts and our unquiet hearts, where do we find the emotional energy to pray?

But God commands that we pray. He didn't make prayer optional; He doesn't hand us a signed excuse releasing us from prayer when life becomes difficult. God must have known that the process of thinking thoughts to an unseen "Something" might seem inadequate in the face of our own suffering, that spending time alone in our room praying the same thing yet again, might seem better spent pacing. He must have known each of us would come to the difficult day when, faced with the urge or challenge to pray, we would instead say, "I just can't," and go no further.

In obedience to God's command, prayer must become what Oswald Chambers called "an effort of the will." When life is difficult, any effort can seem like too much. But if we explore ways of praying that may be easier with limited physical and emotional strength, we more readily may set our wills in the direction of prayer.

## Find a Prayerful Place

Jesus often went to solitary places to pray, such as the mountaintop, the lake, and the garden (see Matt. 14:23; 26:36-46; Mark 1:35; and John 6:22-24.) We can't always arrange a trip to a mountaintop, but we can find somewhere appealing to pray. Slip into a church sanctuary and look at the cross or stained-glass windows. Spend a quiet hour at a museum. Create a prayerful place in your home by lighting a candle or placing your chair by the window. Or simply go for a walk.

## Use Others' Words

When our prayers need words we can't seem to find, we can use someone else's. The Bible is filled with prayers. Consider the petitions of Moses as he struggled to lead God's people. Listen to the kings of Israel as they prayed for help in battle. Borrow the words of the psalmists as they prayed for deliverance, protection, and forgiveness. In the New Testament, meditate on the words of Jesus and the apostles.

For example, consider the prayer of King Jehoshaphat. A messenger greeted him with these words: "A vast army is coming against you" (2 Chron. 20:2). The future of his kingdom was in peril; he and his people were trapped by mighty opponents. The king listened to this message and then prayed: "We have no power to face this vast army that is attacking us. We do not know what to do, but our eyes are upon you" (v. 12). I've borrowed these words of the besieged king when I've felt overpowered by circumstances outside of my control. His prayer is like a flare shot up to the God who rescues.

Consider using other written prayers as well, such as the words from hymns or from a book of prayers.

## Meditate on Jesus' Life

Jesus had a hard life. Can we find something in His life that mirrors our own difficult times? The Gospels tell us about the time He prayed alone at night, so full of emotion that He sweat drops of blood. We can read about the betrayal by His friends and the religious establishment. We can wonder how He must have suffered over being misunderstood by His family.

Did He feel sorrow when He was rebuked rather than praised for performing a miracle? What was He thinking as He wept over His friend Lazarus's grave? How did He find the strength to put one foot in front of the other on the way to His own crucifixion? Can we relate to His cry on the cross, "My God, my God, why have you forsaken me?" (Matt. 27:46).

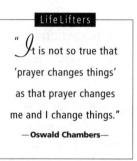

### LifeLifters

" $\mathcal{I}$ t is not so true that 'prayer changes things' as that prayer changes me and I change things."

—**Oswald Chambers**—

Feeling scared and cowardly when I needed to be calm and brave, I thought about Jesus entering Jerusalem for the last time before His death. Even knowing what was ahead, Jesus walked right into His crisis. Horribly unfair things were about to happen to Him. Humiliation and death awaited. If He could walk into that, then with His strength, I could walk into the experience I was facing.

As we meditate upon Jesus' life in this way, we connect with Him and share our experience with Him. This too is a way of praying.

## Pray a Repeated Phrase

It can also be helpful to pray often using the same few words. These words can be prayed aloud, whispered, or said inwardly while engaged in another activity.

There is no magic in the repetition of these words. Rather, what you're seeking is a continual prayer, a constant reminder of the truth to which you so desperately need to cling, a focus for unfocused thoughts. The sudden onsets of panic and grief after the loss of my baby eased when I repeated Jesus' words over and over again: "Peace I leave with you; my peace I give you" (John 14:27).

## Remember the Holy Spirit's Intercession

The advocacy of the Holy Spirit on our behalf is unceasing. Paul tells us that the Holy Spirit prays for us when we are weak, when we don't even know how to pray or what to pray for (see Rom. 8:26-27).

Just as a bewildered plaintiff or defendant—without ability to plead his own case before a judge and jury—asks an attorney to speak for him, so we can entrust our cause to the Holy Spirit and remain silent for a time. This silence does not imply a lack of interest in being before God but rather a choice to be represented by the petitions of the Holy Spirit.

## Assume a Posture of Prayer

There is a good reason for the traditional prayer posture of closed hands and eyes: the less we see and touch, the more we focus on praying. But when our hearts and minds are racing, even this traditional prayer posture can be inadequate to help us focus. Sometimes, we may need a more intentional posture, such as kneeling or even lying prostrate on the floor. With our faces to the floor, we find ourselves in the company of others who have cried out to God from this position: Ezekiel, in despair; Ezra, ashamed and disgraced; Daniel, terrified; Jesus, sorrowful and troubled.

## Write It Once

Simply thinking about our problems before praying may emotionally exhaust or dredge up resentment or anger. When I described to a friend my struggle to pray about a difficult situation, she advised me to write out a prayer that covered all the aspects of the problem. Then she suggested I read this prayer whenever I felt the need to pray, focusing my heart and mind on the words I'd already written. What a relief it was to have a plan for prayer, so I wouldn't need to search the pain daily, starting from scratch.

## Show, Don't Tell

When Sennacherib sent a letter to King Hezekiah threatening to destroy Jerusalem, Hezekiah read it and immediately went to the temple. He spread the letter out before the Lord and began to pray (see 2 Kings 19). Could our prayers be supported by a visual aid as well? By using images rather than words, we can bypass the energy needed to find the words. With one action we can lay our situation before the God who sees as well as hears. Spread the stack of bills, the anti-depressant prescription, or the abnormal biopsy report before Him. Tell God by showing God.

## Pray with Your Tears

Mary wept at Jesus' feet after the death of her brother, Lazarus (see John 11:32-33). Can you recall a time when you cried with another person? Do you remember the emotional release and subsequent bonding with that person after the tears? We can open our hearts to God and deepen our relationship with Him by crying in His presence, offering our tears as prayers.

## Express Your Anger

Anger blocks communication. Are you angry at God over your situation? If so, tell Him how you feel. Follow Job's example of talking to God with honesty and respect. Talk it out, write it down, and watch for His answer.

## Be Silent

Only the best of friends can sit together silently with ease. The psalmist reminds us to "be still, and know that I am God" (Ps. 46:10) and reassures us that "the Lord Almighty is with us" (v. 11). Allow yourself to sit silently in the presence of God.

## Ask Others to Pray

To release God's power on the battlefield below, Moses' friends helped him hold up his staff (Exod. 17:8-13). In the same way, the prayers of others support us and release the power of God into the battles of our lives. If you don't know of at least one person who is committed to praying for you, ask someone.

As I stared out the window in that hospital room, I had a definite sense of others praying for me. My loneliness eased and the struggle to pray relaxed. I didn't have to search for the words anymore; I knew the words of someone else would bring me before God.

## Do You Believe?

At the memorial service we held for our infant daughter, we read the words spoken by Jesus to a grieving Martha four days after the death of her brother. Jesus said to her: "I am the resurrection and the life .... Do you believe this?" Martha replied, "Yes, Lord" (John 11:25-27). Jesus then proceeded to the tomb, twice overcome with emotion before arriving. Moments later Lazarus walked out of the tomb, resurrected.

Despair and belief, sorrow and joy, death and life, waiting and rescue are the threads woven together in the fabric of this story. They are also the fabric of my story and perhaps yours. As with Martha, our hope when life gets hard rests in the way we answer Jesus' question: "I am the resurrection and the life. Do you believe this?" If we can say yes, no matter how we choose to pray about the difficulties we face, we know that we leave our prayers in trustworthy hands.

# chapter three

# Why Won't I Pray with
## *My Wife?*

Breaking Barriers to Spiritual Intimacy

### *Dr. Louis McBurney*

*A* sick feeling takes over the pit of my stomach. The pastor's wife I'm counseling has just brought up a topic I'd rather avoid. Nancy is registering her hurt at the hands of her pastor-husband—and nailing me in the process.

"I remember how excited I was when we fell in love, and I realized I was going to be married to a minister," she says. "I had always prayed for a godly husband, a man who would be a spiritual leader for me and our children. I was sure Joe would be God's answer to those prayers. We even prayed together on our dates. It gave me such a secure feeling.

"I just don't know what happened. After we married all of that stopped. Oh, sometimes we still pray together or read the Bible, but only if I insist. That doesn't feel right. I want him to take the leadership for our spiritual life together."

I'm gulping hard and nodding knowingly—too knowingly. I've heard my wife echo similar concerns. One of my frequent failures: not taking initiative for *spiritual closeness in marriage.*

*Why is spiritual intimacy with my wife so easy to avoid?*

## Reasonable Excuses

I've discovered I'm not alone. Most of the ministers we counsel at Marble Retreat also struggle with this problem. Some common explanations have emerged.

The first is the professional exhaustion defense. It goes something like this: "I have to keep up this mask of religiosity almost all the time. From morning till night I'm the minister. I can't just be me. I'm always the one called on to pray everywhere I go. The only other guy who's prayed at Kiwanis in the past four years is Father O'Roarke. Men in the locker room at the health club apologize for cussing in front of me. I'm always expected to have Scriptural answers for every question and deliver them with a loving smile.

"I get sick of it. Home is the only place I can relax and be real. I want to share spiritual things with my wife, but quite frankly, when she says, 'Can't we pray together?' I feel attacked. Then I feel guilty. Then I feel angry. Then I just want to escape."

I can't use this excuse, however; I'm a shrink, not a man of the cloth.

The second excuse, the hypocrisy factor, does fit me. My wife, Melissa, sees me offering sound spiritual counsel to others, but she knows I'm no saint. Sometimes I'm reluctant to pray with my wife because of this rationale: "Melissa knows the real me. It's fine to offer holy solutions and wise biblical advice to others, but I can't get away with that at home. She knows I'm not very disciplined. She's seen my temper. She puts up with my pouts.

"She remembers the ways I've hurt her through the years by my selfishness or lust or thoughtless actions. She knows what I've been like as a father to our children. I'd feel like a total hypocrite expounding some Scripture to her or offering some pious prayer. She'd crucify me.

"No, it's safer to just play the game. She knows me too well. Maybe someday when I get my act together ...."

Of course, the problem with that is I'll never get my act together. I need at least one place I can let down and be real. That seems more necessary than devotions.

The third factor is the spiritual dwarf syndrome. Many ministers believe, often accurately, that their spouse is a spiritual giant compared to themselves. They feel dwarfed by her deep faith. She doesn't seem to agonize with the same gut-wrenching doubts and questions as he.

Her quietly committed prayer life shines compared to his hasty, often desperate prayers fired off on the run. The Word seems to speak to her. Ages have passed since he has even read the Scriptures to find God's message for himself, and she wants him to be her "spiritual leader?"

How can he risk the vulnerability that spiritual union would bring? She'd find out how shallow he really is. He feels less dwarfish behind the pulpit. Better stay there. It's definitely safer.

## Holy Disharmony

Another obstacle to spiritual intimacy is holy disharmony. Distinctive belief differences or style preferences may create dissonance when you try to pray, worship, or interpret Scripture together. Rather than unifying, it divides. You both agree with Paul that your joy would be complete if you were only of one mind, but that's about all you agree on. Common areas of disagreement include preference for time of day, interpretation of Scripture, devotional style, and issues of trust.

Melissa is a morning person, for example. For her, the most meaningful devotional experiences are flooded by the first rays of the rising sun. I'm pretty convinced, however, that God doesn't wake up till mid afternoon. I'm sure the splendor of starlight was created to bathe our expressions of worship. That difference seems trivial until we try to adjust our biological clocks to find time for devotional togetherness.

If your devotional time together includes reading Scripture, you may find tension in how you interpret what you read. One of you may thoroughly enjoy lively debate, discussing various interpretations. The other may shrink from such encounters, preferring to find a practical application or an inspiring devotional thought. It is easy for a win-lose dynamic to emerge that quickly poisons the wellspring of shared spirituality.

Another difference is style. When praying together, this includes the volume of words, the use of the language of Zion versus the vernacular, who does the praying, what resources are chosen, and what physical posture is preferred. If our mate's style is too divergent from our own, the feeling of genuine contact with God may be destroyed.

A friend of mine told me once that he couldn't pray with his wife. By the time they finished, he felt his prayer had been rated like an Olympic diver. He usually got only about a 6.0. His wife went on to a 9.5 performance.

## Digging Out

So what's to be done? Most clergy couples agree they need the sense of spiritual oneness. Wives particularly crave the feeling of closeness nurtured in those moments of bondedness before the Lord. Avoidance or a frustrated acceptance of failure doesn't bring much peace.

You don't have to remain stuck, though, in the ditch of spiritual estrangement. Here are some steps Melissa and I have found helpful for ourselves and others.

**1. Identify the problem.**

Clear an afternoon or evening in your schedule to discuss this area of your relationship. Allow no interruptions, and covenant together to make understanding (not agreement) your goal. Enter the time without your usual agenda of proving who's right and who's wrong. Believe me, you both are right *and* wrong.

Trace the history of your spiritual relationship, recalling the times it went well and the times it didn't work for you. Then try to identify how you've felt inside about having a time of spiritual conversation.

Try not to let "time demands" be the rationalization. As difficult as it is, I find most people make time for the things that reward them. Push beyond your busy schedules, and search for deeper problems.

Your goal is to understand each other in a non-judgmental way. You may be uncomfortable with how your mate feels, but accept her perception as the truth from which she acts.

## 2. Clarify expectations.

I used to believe Melissa wanted me to be something I'm not. She would talk about her desire for me to be more of a spiritual leader for her. That sounded pretty overwhelming to me. So rather than risk embarrassment or failure, I'd avoid even trying. I interpreted her expectations as wanting me to lead in deep discussion of the Scriptures or to expound or some dramatic vision the Lord had given me (a fresh one for each day, of course).

When I finally told her what I thought she craved, she was flabbergasted. I'll never forget the relief I felt when she said, "Oh, that's not what I want. I just want a spiritual companion, not a leader."

Often our expectations are totally unrealistic or simply indescribably vague. We may have developed an image of what spiritual sharing is supposed to look like from some conference or a book we read, but never stopped to define it clearly with our mate.

## 3. Re-negotiate a contract.

When I had a clearer idea of Melissa's expectations, I felt more comfortable working toward an agreement. What would "spiritual companionship" look like to her? What were specific things I could do that would invite her into my soul-life?

As it turned out, what she'd been wanting was much easier than what I'd been assuming. We began to spend a short time at breakfast reading Scripture (usually a paragraph or maybe a chapter), then praying together briefly about our individual concerns. It also helps when I talk about how the Lord is working in my heart. At times we get together for a longer period of prayer or discussion, usually when life's pressures seem to be closing in.

**4. Avoid criticism.**

You can be pretty sure that you're going to blow it somewhere along the way. You'll get busy or be angry with each other or somebody will have the flu, and then you won't do it the way you intended. When that happens, refuse to place blame and judgment *anywhere*. That's deadly.

**5. Celebrate your steps toward spiritual oneness.**

Every time Melissa tells me how good she feels when I initiate sharing, I get a renewed commitment to the process. Our unity is reinforced each time we tell others about the importance of having a soul mate as our spouse—for example, when we're with friends and I tell them that Melissa and I were praying together for them the other day, or when she says, "Louis and I were just reading that Scripture recently."

Those comments are ways we let each other know how satisfying our spiritual closeness is.

Ours has been a rocky pilgrimage in this area. But we're finding a new sense of freedom and safety. Our growing spiritual oneness is helping us enjoy more fully the other dimensions of our lives together, whether long walks hand in hand or our sexual intimacy. It's still not easy, but the strength and joy we experience together makes the struggle worthwhile.

# chapter four

# Praying below the
# *Surface*

How Paul prayed for spiritual needs.

*Pamela Binkley*

*A*s I prayed, I knew something was missing. Requests from the women in my Bible study group had grown predictable. Concerns about health, careers, cantankerous cars, financial needs, and trying relationships packed my prayer journal. I'd even prayed about two leaky roofs.

*Shouldn't there be requests for spiritual needs?* I wondered. Not that the prayers in my journal were insignificant. Along with the other women, I'd learned by His answers that God's love for us and the ingenuity of His solutions to our problems defy the imagination. He tends to our daily needs even as He tends to our souls. Besides, one of those leaky roofs was mine!

But were there other prayers God wanted me to offer up for these women? The answer surfaced the year our leader challenged us: "As you study the letters of Paul, look for the prayers he prayed for the churches and pray each one for your group."

My first discovery occurred in 1 Thessalonians

5:23—a petition for purity. I knelt and asked, "May the spirit, soul, and body of each woman be kept blameless at the coming of our Lord Jesus Christ." Surely, this prayer was holy to God. I began to understand that God wants us to pray for daily needs, but He also wants us to pray for our spiritual needs.

Here are some of the prayers I found as I continued scouting Paul's epistles. Pray them for your small group, your Sunday school class, your friends, or your family. Put them in your own words. Identify what keeps us from enjoying these spiritual qualities and ask God to remove those hindrances.

## A Prayer for Filling and Spilling

"May the God of hope fill you with all joy and peace as you trust in him, so that you may overflow with hope by the power of the Holy Spirit" (Rom. 15:13).

I pray that the women in my group will know this kind of trust in God, and will act on His promises. One woman did just that when she felt vulnerable to a temptation. A man she knew kept calling her when her husband was out of town. She asked God to remove the temptation those phone calls represented, based on His promise not to tempt us beyond what we are able to withstand. The next time her husband went out of town, she discovered she could make outgoing calls, but couldn't receive incoming ones. God kept her tempter from calling at a time when she felt weak.

What are the enemies of trust? Pessimism, fearfulness, and timidity all threaten our ability to trust God. So I pray for confidence and courage. What keeps your group or family from trusting God?

## A Prayer for Unity

"May the God who gives endurance and encouragement give you a spirit of unity among yourselves as you follow Christ Jesus, so that with one heart and mouth you may glorify the God and Father of our Lord Jesus Christ" (Rom. 15:5-6).

The first night our study group meets in September, I listen to the women introduce themselves and wonder how such a diverse group will bond. They are CPAs, crossing guards, mothers, teachers, physicians, and office workers. Some work fifty-hour weeks; some are retired. They represent different races, marital statuses, incomes, and denominations. One or two may be unchurched. Several talk at the same time. Another sits without saying a word. As I pray Paul's prayer for unity, I ask God to keep our differences from pulling us apart. I pray He'll turn our diversity into zest for getting to know one another. I ask that our focus would be on Him, not ourselves.

It never fails; at some point during the year I look around and see how God has taken all our differences and arranged them in a perfect bouquet. Our dissimilarities blend because we are following Christ. He makes us one with Him and with each other.

## A Prayer to Know God Better

"I keep asking that the God of our Lord Jesus Christ, the glorious Father, may give you the Spirit of wisdom and revelation, so that you may know Him better. I pray also that the eyes of your heart may be enlightened in order that you may know the hope to which he has called you, the riches of his glorious inheritance in the saints, and his incomparably great power for us who believe" (Eph. 1:17-19).

With this prayer as my model, I ask God to free the women in my group from the cobwebs in their thinking. Sometimes the cobwebs are beliefs that God can hardly wait for us to fail so He can punish us. When that's the case, I pray for His love to become a reality. Sometimes the cobwebs are a lack of strength to do the things we want to do. Then I pray for God's power to become real. Years ago, this empowerment enabled me to quit smoking.

In our discussions I listen for words like, "I used to think ...." That's my clue that someone is about to clear out a cobweb and share a newly learned truth.

Key to knowing God is a commitment to read and study Scripture. I pray that each woman will seek out that private place and block of time God has given her. I ask that her time with God would be so rich she will refuse to let the pressures of the day grab it away from her.

I also pray that as each woman becomes familiar with Scripture she will not stop learning about God— that none of us will ever settle back with an I-have-arrived attitude. As we continue to see how great God is, we must surely see how minuscule our godliness and our knowledge is in comparison.

## A Prayer for Salt-and-Light Love

"And this is my prayer: that your love may abound more and more in knowledge and depth of insight, so that you may be able to discern what is best and may be pure and blameless until the day of Christ, filled with the fruit of righteousness that comes through Jesus Christ—to the glory and praise of God" (Phil. 1:9-11).

I ask God to instill in our group of women a love for others like Christ's love for us. This love is more than a pat on the back and a smile for one who is deeply distressed. Rather it is a love that sits down and listens. It is a love that empathizes and encourages, it's a salt-and-light love that speaks what is true. When it offers advice, that counsel comes from a storage bin of Christ's wisdom.

Such love points others toward Christ instead of trying to garner glory for itself. It is a love that sometimes surprises, because it loves even those who are not so easy to love. Pray that your group will see others with the eyes of Christ. Pray that their love will be fruitful because it points others toward God. Pray they will love even when the object of their love doesn't deserve it, acknowledging that Christ's love too is undeserved.

## A Prayer for Sharing Faith

"I pray that you may be active in sharing your faith, so that you will have a full understanding of every good thing we have in Christ" (Philemon 6).

We share our faith by telling and doing. I pray that the women in my group will share their faith in both these ways, and that as they do, their faith will become more real to them.

I also pray that we will tell others about our faith. Timidity often hinders us from sharing, so I pray for the courage to speak out. Caring about what others think is another hindrance to witnessing, so I pray we will not be influenced by what people think of us.

## More Than Meets the Eye

The answers to prayers like these are not as tangible as the answers to prayers about cantankerous cars and leaky roofs. Sometimes the answers are long in coming. Spiritual qualities, like oak trees, take time to mature. Sometimes the answers are hidden from us because they represent private victories. If you become discouraged because you don't see the results of your spiritual petitions, ask God to let you see just enough so that you will persevere.

When I'm inclined to lose heart in prayer, I picture the Old Testament high priests. They entered the Holy of Holies, bearing the names of the twelve tribes of Israel carved on stones and worked into the breastplate. Because of Jesus, each of us is now a priest. We too can enter the Holy of Holies, carrying the names of those we pray for and equipped with model prayers from Paul.

# chapter five

# Praying for Your *Husband*

Making a difference in ministry.

*Bette Morgan*

*I* was reflecting on the past twenty-five years of serving the Lord with my husband in the pastorate and ways in which I perhaps had "made a difference." Though many of those years involved raising our five children, we pastored four churches, and then served four years in ministry to seminary students and wives. Now the Lord has given me the opportunity to serve as Director of Women's Ministries on the staff of a large church where my husband is an associate pastor.

As significant as these ministries seem to be, nevertheless, I am convinced that the most important ministry that assuredly makes a difference is the ministry of praying for my husband.

Any ministry wife in her right mind is praying for her husband, out of sheer desperation if nothing else! However, I challenge you to make a new commitment to spend a certain amount of time in prayer each day just for your husband (five minutes ... ten minutes?). You know him better than anyone else in the whole world (even his mother), and you are best equipped to pray specifically and consistently for him. This is one of the most crucial ways you can really function as a helpmate to him, and the more you pray for him, the more aware you become of practical ways in which you can help and encourage him to be the man God has called him to be.

I offer the following guidelines in the hopes of encouraging other ministry wives in the less visible but most fruitful "difference-making." These are very basic and general, yet specific, prayer requests arranged in a weekly format which has been helpful to me. Personalize and add to the list as only you can for your own husband. The list can also be used as a guideline in praying for other leaders in your churches.

## Weekly Prayer Guide

### *Sunday*

1. That he might have grace and function in preaching, teaching, and prayer; that he might be given utterance in the opening of his mouth to make known with boldness and clarity the mystery of Christ (Col. 4:3-4; Eph. 6:19-20).

2. That, as he leads others in worship and adoration of God, he himself would be biblical and faithful in public and private worship, delighting more and more in God and His Word (Ps. 1:2; 37:4; 119:24, 77, 92, 143; Prov. 23:26; Song 2:3).

3. That he might become a holy man, a humble man of prayer, mature in the Lord, ever growing in his knowledge of God (1 Thess. 5:23; Col. 4:12; Eph. 6:18; 3:16-19; 2 Peter 3:18).

### *Monday*

4.   That he would be able to "relax" (physically, mentally, emotionally) and "unwind" without sinning against God; that he would continually live what he professes, and practice what he preaches (Ps. 101:2-3).

5.   That he might learn and be enabled to make every thought captive, to be not conformed to the world's thinking but to think scripturally (Rom. 12:1-2; 2 Cor. 10:5).

6.   That he would learn to not depend upon his circumstances, people, or things for happiness and fulfillment, but on God alone; that he would consistently feed upon God's Word for the nourishment of his own soul and not merely for preparation of sermons and classes (Hab. 3:17-19; Jer. 15:16).

### *Tuesday*

7.   That he might daily seek God with all of his heart, walking in the Spirit moment by moment in a manner worthy of the Lord, growing in his trust in and dependence on Him (Ps. 63:1-2; 119:1-2; 27:4; Prov. 3:5-6; John 15:5).

8.   That his sense of significance and self-image would be a reflection of the Lord's thoughts toward him (Eph. 1:17-18; Rom. 12:3; Ps. 139).

9.   That he might have new, increased strength in the midst of his busy schedule; that the Lord would infuse him to labor faithfully in his appointed place of service (Isa. 40-31; Eph. 3:14-19; Phil. 4:13).

### *Wednesday*

10. That he would be faithful as a pastor-teacher to "equip the saints for the work of service, to the

building up of the body of Christ" so that all the members of the congregation would attain maturity, unity of faith, and the knowledge of Christ (Eph. 4:11-13).

11. That God would enable him to be faithful and fruitful in training leadership, by precept and example, for the building and strengthening of God's kingdom (1 Tim. 4:11-12; Eph. 5:1-2).

12. That he might learn to love God and others in a biblical way, acquiring and demonstrating a shepherd's heart for all the flock with whom God has made him "overseer" (1 Cor. 13:4-7; Rom. 12:8-10; Acts 20:28).

### *Thursday*

13. That he might demonstrate reverence and gratitude as a called man, not driven, with well-thought-through and prayed-through goals in life, always in the context of his mission (1 Cor. 9:19-27).

14. That the Lord would give him wisdom to lead his family physically, emotionally, mentally, and spiritually; that he would lovingly give teaching, exhortation, encouragement, and discipline as needed (Eph. 1:17, 19; 6:4; 5:25-31; 1 Thess. 2:11-12; James 1:5-7).

15. That the fruit of the Spirit might be exhibited more and more in his life (Gal. 5:22-23).

### *Friday*

16. That he might stand firm against the schemes of the devil, recognizing and resisting Satan in all circumstances (Eph. 6:10-18; James 4:7; 2 Cor. 2:11; 1 Peter 5:8).

17. That he might not be deceived into unbelief

or sin in any form; that he would be uncompromising with the world, the flesh, and the devil (Matt. 26:58-75; Gal. 6:7; Eph. 5:11).

18. That he would be continually faithful to examine himself in light of Scripture, recognizing, confessing, and repenting all inward and outward sins (Ps. 119:130; 32:1-5; 51:10; 1 John 1:7, 9).

### Saturday

19. That the Lord would protect him, guarding his course; that he would have needful grace to accept all "disappointments" as God's sovereign appoint-ments, submitting cheerfully and trustfully to the Lordship of Christ in his life (Prov. 2:8; 19:21; 2 Thess. 3:3; Ps. 135:6; Eph. 1:11; Dan. 4:35).

20. That he might be self-disciplined, learning to manage his time well (Eph. 5:15; Phil. 2:12-13).

21. That as God continues to give him favor with his own flock, so He would give him favor with others outside the walls of the church, opening doors of opportunity for him to have a godly influence in the community in evangelism and discipleship (Ps. 133:1-3; Prov. 21:1; Neh. 1:11; 2:18, 20).

"Now to Him who is able to do exceedingly abundantly beyond all that we ask or think, according to the power that works within us, to Him be glory in the church by Christ Jesus to all generations, forever and ever. Amen" (Eph. 3:20-21, NKJV).

# chapter six

# *Leading* on Your Knees

The prayer life of the leader.

*Shelly Esser*

*H*ow many hours in the past year did you spend in prayer for your husband, your congregation, your ministry area, the people under your leadership? When was the last time you were on your knees for the leadership in your church and the many concerns that face the ministry? Perhaps the greatest weakness of the church today is the lack of intercession by the leaders for their people.

So what should be the role of prayer in your life as a leader or co-partner in ministry? It should be the same as the apostles gave in Acts 6:4, "... And will give our attention to prayer and the ministry of the word." Prayer was the apostles' first priority; it took up the largest amount of their time. And as was so evident in their ministries, they could only lead as they prayed— and the same is true for us.

Since my husband's resignation as associate pastor a little over a year ago, I've had a lot of time to reflect on the ministry we had—what was good, what was bad, and what things I'd do differently if given the opportunity. At the top of my list of things I'd change, is my own prayerlessness in regard to our ministry. In fact, I have been deeply grieved by my omission in this area.

We had always heard coming into ministry that relationships are often the first place the enemy will strike to dismantle a work. I believed it, I had even witnessed it before, but I never thought it would happen to us, especially coming into a church on the tails of a church split where relationships had already been fragmented and attacked. "Surely it won't happen again," I reasoned.

As a result, I didn't bother to pray for protection or for the relationships among the staff; in fact, I didn't pray much at all, at least not about the important things. I became overly confident, neglecting the place and power of prayer in our ministry lives.

A soldier would never think of stepping into the front lines of battle unequipped or unprepared; you can bet he would have all of the necessary weaponry needed to wage the battle he was engaging in. Yet as leaders in the church, stepping daily onto the enemy's battlefield, we naively think we can do it alone, or do it without the weapon of prayer, and so we mistakenly let our guards down. Scripture tells us over and over again, the battle we are engaged in is not a battle with human flesh but against the darkness and principalities of this world. Yet we aren't watchful and prayerful as we're so adamantly instructed to be.

One of our greatest offensive weapons in battle is prayer; but unfortunately, all too often, we use it as a last resort or not at all. Unfortunately many churches are full of the casualties of war and destructive forces operating beneath the surface because of our neglect.

I don't know if the outcome of our situation might have changed as a result of intercession, but I do believe that many things in the church could have been different and that God's power could have been unleashed in many ways if we, as leaders, would have regularly come together in prayer for each other and the flock. I am convinced that there would be less complaining, disunity, bitter roots, criticism, fleshly behavior, and the quenching and grieving of the Holy Spirit in a praying church. First Thessalonians 5:19 tells us, "Do not put out the Spirit's fire." A sure way to quench that fire in a church is prayerlessness and self-reliance.

A Christian writer once proposed this question: "What if there are some things God will not do until people pray?" A very challenging and sobering question. That question has haunted me many times as I have looked back and reflected on my own prayerlessness. God has made us active participants in the fulfillment of His kingdom and will through prayer, yet how often we fail to respond in this privileged way.

E.M. Bounds said, "Each leader must be preeminently a man of prayer. His heart must graduate in the school of prayer. No earnestness, no diligence, no study, no gifts will supply its lack. Talking to men for God is a great thing, but talking to God for men is greater still. He will never talk well and with real success to men for God who has not learned well how to talk to God for men." One of the reasons so many Christian workers today have such little influence is the prayerlessness of their service. To effectively learn how to pray and be empowered by the Holy Spirit and guided through prayer is the most important task in our preparation as leaders.

Think about your individual ministry or church for a minute. What do you spend most of your time on as a leader? Planning? Publicity? Refreshments? Organization? Delegating? Prayer is often tagged on as an afterthought, isn't it? Prayer must be the foundation of all we do or we're building our ministries and churches on sand. All

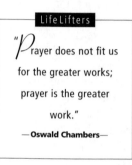

successes apart from the spiritual empowerment and touch of the Holy Spirit, is a house or ministry or church built on sand—and when the winds come it will fall; it won't last. I wonder how many church splits and discords have been birthed in prayerlessness?

Wesley Duewel said, "You will never be a greater leader than your prayers. Effectiveness in leadership is dependent on our spiritual life, on our prayer life. Our very usefulness is dependent on prayer. It is prayer that prepares us for every aspect of the work because spiritual ministry demands spiritual power not ministry done in the flesh. One danger of operating ministry life devoid of prayer is that we become too dependent on the flesh and the methods of the flesh."

It's been said that the Holy Spirit does not flow through methods, but men and women. He does not anoint plans and programs, but men and women. It's very easy, especially over the years, to become too reliant on our own plans and methods. Especially here, we need to be careful that everything we do is God-made and not man-made—that we keep totally dependent on God for the work of the ministry through prayer and the empowerment of the Holy Spirit. As leaders, we need to remain close to God's heart on a daily basis so we're ready and knowledgeable for His marching orders and desires for the ministry He has entrusted to us.

God has given us a great responsibility to intercede for our people. We must pray for our ministry, the services in the church, the outreach, the families, the individuals, and the church at large. First Samuel 12:23 very soberly reminds us, "Far be it from me that I should sin against the Lord by failing to pray for you." Too often we neglect praying for our people and ministry. Personal prayer is to be our daily ministry and work, especially as a Christian leader.

There is no better example in Scripture—besides the Lord Jesus Himself—than the Apostle Paul, when it comes to displaying a model leader's prayer life. Paul was a man who was committed to praying for his people, his coworkers, his brothers and sisters in Christ, and the lost. At least forty-one verses in his writings refer to his prayer and subjects for prayer. His ministry grew out of his unceasing prayer life. It was the very foundation of his ministry and effectiveness as a leader. And as a by-product of his life, he developed a praying people. When we as leaders model prayer in our churches and corners of ministry, it will become contagious.

We are currently attending a church where the pastor has wisely made prayer a central focus of the church. Opportunities for prayer abound everywhere and the amazing thing is people are responding and catching the vision for the need for prayer in their personal lives and the life of the church. Men are coming together regularly to pray for the pastor, the church leadership, and the Spirit's anointing. Exciting things are beginning to happen as a result. People are coming to Christ, and God's people are learning to pray, many for the first time. There is such a spirit of unity, love, and warmth, and the Holy Spirit's presence is so evidently resident in the church—the fruit of a praying church.

What did Paul pray? First, Paul prayed in thanksgiving to God and for the believers he was writing to. What did he pray for these people? He prayed that they would be encouraged. Throughout his letters he continually tells his readers, "I have not stopped praying for you," "I kneel before the Father continually, day and night wrestling in prayer for you." Could it be said of you that you are wrestling in prayer for your people, for your teammates, for your husband?

Additionally, Paul prayed for their perseverance in the faith and ministry, for their empowerment, that they would be active in sharing their faith and for their spiritual growth and witness. The bulk of Paul's prayer life was praying faithfully for others. In Ephesians 1:15-20, he tells the believers this, "For this reason, ever since I heard about your faith in the Lord Jesus and your love for all the saints, I have not stopped giving thanks for you, remembering you in my prayers. I keep asking that the God of our Lord Jesus Christ, the glorious Father may give you the Spirit of wisdom and revelation, so that you may know him better. I pray also that the eyes of your heart may be enlightened in order that you may know the hope to which he has called you, the riches of his glorious inheritance in the saints, and his incomparably great power for us who believe." Wow! I'd love for someone to be praying that kind of prayer on my behalf.

Paul also encouraged the believers to pray for one another. He spoke of this in eight of his letters. As leaders we need each other's intercession, don't we? Again, this is an area I would do over again. I deeply regret not having initiated prayer with our church's other ministry wife. We needed it, our husbands needed it, our children needed it, and the church desperately needed it. We need a ministry prayer partner. If not in your own church, perhaps another ministry wife in a neighboring church would be delighted to have a prayer partner. There is no greater and more comforting way to bear one another's burdens than through prayer. When two or three gather in His name there is power, the Bible tells us in Matthew 18:19-20.

Finally, Paul requested prayer for himself. Very few of Paul's prayers were for himself, but he knew that he was dependent on the prayers of his people. How often have we failed to pray for our leaders because we either thought they didn't need it or surely many others were committed to praying for them? First Timothy 2:1-4 clearly instructs us to pray for all of our leaders. Leaders, especially, need our continual prayers. In Ephesians 6:19-20, Paul says, "Pray also for me, that whenever I open my mouth, words may be given me so that I will fearlessly make known the mystery of the gospel, for which I am an ambassador in chains. Pray that I may declare it fearlessly, as I should."

May the Lord help us to become women of prayer, women who will turn our churches upside down because we have learned to commune regularly with the Master.

## Practical Suggestions for Becoming a Praying Leader

1.    Evaluate your current prayer life, gauge where changes need to be made and make a new commitment to the Lord today to either begin anew, or improve and extend what you have already been doing.

2.    Plan your prayer time for your husband, church, and leaders. Reserve a special daily or weekly time for praying very specifically for these needs. As a leader, your people should constantly be on your heart, just as Paul's were.

3.    Have a place where you can pray for them. You need a prayer closet (room, chair, car, shower, someplace where you can regularly pray for their needs). Use a prayer list. God greatly blesses the use of prayer lists. There is great evidence that Paul used them. If your church has a pictorial or non-pictorial church directory, this is an excellent way to pray by name, for your people.

4.    Plan how you will cover the needs of your church and people. Plan ways to pray regularly for all of the people, especially for whom you are spiritually responsible and accountable to God. Try to keep this list updated. Remember you can bear burdens for one

another through prayer. Other things to cover in your prayer time might include: unity, integrity, godly living, a praying people (which by the way, is modeled by the leadership of the church), a witnessing people, revival, a growing, healthy church, to name a few.

5.    If you have a difficult time verbalizing exactly what to pray for your leaders, use some of Paul's prayers found in his letters. Make them your own, praying his requests for your own leaders. Praying Scripture into people's lives, is a great basis for prayer. (Start with 1 Thess. 1:2-3; Phil. 1:4-6; Eph. 1:15-20.)

6.    Find a prayer partner, either in your own church or a ministry wife in another church.

# chapter seven

# What's My *Story?*

## *Lydia E. Harris*

*Y*ears before my birth, God began weaving the fabric of my life with vibrant threads of prayer. Without those threads, I would not have been born. In 1929, Nicolai Siemens was imprisoned in Moscow's dreaded Lubjanka Prison, awaiting deportation to Siberia because he was a minister of the Gospel.

Meanwhile, in Chicago, Illinois, his older brother picked up the *Chicago Daily Tribune* and read, "Russia Deports 2,000 Germans to Siberia Camps." Sensing his brother Nicolai was among them, he felt burdened to hold a prayer vigil, entreating God for Nicolai's release.

The Pilgrims' Mission Church was filled with sixty kneeling prayer warriors, interceding into the night until my uncle announced, "We can stop now. I have the conviction God has answered our prayers." Indeed God had answered, and during the same hour, the man who became my father was miraculously released to be reunited with his wife and newborn son. Within days they exited Moscow's Red Gate on a train to freedom.

My family later immigrated to Blaine, Washington. By 1944, the family had grown to five daughters and two sons. My mother, forty-four, was content with her large family and didn't want any surprise additions. But her daughters were praying for a baby sister. Soon, used baby clothes were laundered and hung on the clothesline, announcing my mother's pregnancy.

As the birth approached, my brothers predicted, "It's going to be a boy; we already have too many girls."

"Did you pray about it?" the girls questioned. The boys hung their heads sheepishly.

"We did, and we prayed for a girl!" exclaimed my sisters confidently. I'm thankful to be the answer to their prayers.

My life was further woven by the fervent prayers of godly parents, interceding daily for my siblings and me. As a result, I accepted the Lord as a preschooler and learned the value of prayer through family devotions and my parents' example. I later married a Christian and we raised a daughter and son.

Then came 1988, a year of great change in my life. Within six months, both of my aging parents died and our firstborn left for college. I felt the loss of my parents' prayers and asked, "Who will pray for us now?" God answered through *Moms In Touch*, an international organization of mothers praying for their children and schools. I found kindred hearts to join me in prayer for my children.

Nine years later, I see the ripple effect of prayer. Not only did prayer change me, but my entire family. My husband and I now pray together regularly and are involved in a church prayer ministry. Both our children are walking with God and have a heart for prayer. Our extended family (siblings and their families) has met regularly for five years to pray for family needs. Though we've faced struggles like illness, alcoholism, and divorce, we've rejoiced in God's blessings of healing, godly marriages, and new births—both physical and spiritual. We continue to reap the fruit of my parents' faithful prayers. As we follow their example, our prayers are the lasting threads woven into the fabric of future generations.

"I will sing of the mercies of the LORD forever; with my mouth will I make known Your faithfulness through all generations" (Ps. 89:1, NKJV).

Lydia E. Harris

# chapter eight

# Digging Deeper:

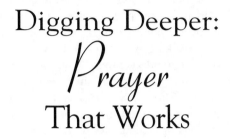

That Works

*Elizabeth Greene*

S o often when it comes to prayer we spend most of
our time reading books or sharing requests and
relatively little time in actual conversation with our
Heavenly Father.

In Old Testament times, only the High Priest could
enter into God's presence in the Holy of Holies. He
went in just once a year and never went in without
blood. Do you remember what happened when Jesus
died on the cross, paying the price for our sin? Mark
15:38 tells us that the temple curtain ripped in two from
top to bottom. We no longer need a high priest to go
into God's presence to atone for our sins. Jesus paid the
debt. Now, amazingly, we can approach God's throne
of grace with confidence because of the blood of Christ.

Behold what manner of love God has lavished on
us that we can be called His children and dwell in His
presence. Let us spend the next few minutes drawing
near to God in prayer.

I find it easy to bring my long list of requests to
God. But Psalm 100:4 says to "enter his gates with

thanksgiving and his courts with praise." Hebrews 13:15 says, "let us continually offer to God a sacrifice of praise." I find it best to begin prayer with praise because it readjusts my focus from self to Savior. Praise puts life back into perspective.

## Praise

Praise focuses on the character of God—WHO He is. Many psalms describe His marvelous attributes.

Read the following passages of Scripture and meditate on these attributes of God. Then praise God for His holiness based on what you have read:

- Psalm 100
- Psalm 8:1
- Exodus 15:11,13
- Revelation 15:3-4
- What did you learn about God's love and faithfulness from Psalm 100? What implication does this have for your life? Praise Him for this.

## Confession

"Let us examine our ways and test them, and let us return to the LORD. Let us lift up our hearts and our hands to God in heaven and say: We have sinned" (Lam. 3:40-41). After praise comes confession. Take time to ask God to search your heart and bring to mind any actions, thoughts, or motives that would be displeasing to Him. Be specific.

- Why do you think we need to confess our sins to God? Read Psalm 66:18-20 and write down your answer.
- Once we confess our sin to God, what happens? Read 1 John 1:9 and write down your response.

## Prayer

### *Kind and Merciful God*

(Fred Bock Music Company, 1973)
*Kind and merciful God*
*In Christ's death on the cross,*
*You provided a cleansing from sin.*
*Speak the words that forgive,*
*That henceforth we may live*
*By the might of your Spirit within.*

## Thanksgiving

After we have praised God for WHO He is and confessed our sins, we want to thank Him for WHAT He has done.

- Read Psalm 40:5 and 52:9
- What things has God done in your life that you can be thankful for? Be specific! God has blessed us in a variety of ways:
- Material—food, clothing, shelter
- Physical—health or grace in the midst of sickness
- Relational—friends, family, neighbors
- Spiritual—forgiveness of sins, eternal life, Holy Spirit

Thank God for what He had done for you in each category. "Give thanks to the LORD, for he is good; his love endures forever" (Ps. 106:1).

## Requests

"In the morning, O LORD, you hear my voice; in the morning I lay my requests before you and wait in expectation" (Ps. 5:3).

Now that we have spent time focused on God's

character and His works, we can bring forward our requests. Often my list has changed as I meditate on the Lord. Let us pray expectantly, knowing that God hears and answers our prayers. Pray for:

- Friends and family who have not yet crossed the line of faith
- Your own spiritual growth and development (grow in the fruit of the spirit, deepen in your understanding and application of God's Word, recognize and resist temptation, and so forth)
- Your spiritual service (God will use you to further the work of His kingdom)
- Evangelism (that you will be salt and light to a lost world)
- Your list!

Don't get discouraged at the number of requests you have. Rotate what you pray for each day so that it doesn't become burdensome. Enjoy your time of fellowship with God and don't forget to celebrate when you see Him answer requests.

Stay fervent in prayer and "let us hold unswervingly to the hope we profess, for he who promised is faithful" (Heb. 10:23). May God richly bless your life and ministry, as you stay connected to the Lord in prayer.

# chapter nine

# Counseling Corner:
## *The Female*
## Cardinal Syndrome

*Ingrid Lawrenz, MSW*

At a garden party one crisp, sunny spring day, my guests were commenting on the numerous active birds in the yard. They knew I was an amateur naturalist, so they were seeking me out to make identifications. There were playful warblers, chickadees and finches, the calm morning doves, the noisy grackles, and proud woodpeckers. However, suddenly, with a knowing cheer of delight, we all saw and recognized a brilliant red cardinal alight on the cedar tree. This popular bird has often adorned greeting cards, calendars, and paintings. He needed no introduction. Someone then casually queried if that brownish bird feeding on the ground was a large sparrow. Actually, the bright male had taken all the attention away from his lovely bride—the female cardinal. God did not make all birds this way. The sexes of the robins, blue jays, and even parakeets are indistinguishable by color; but for some species the ornate males lure the attention of predators away from the nests. That color also serves to enhance their courtship rituals!

Later that summer a fellow ministry wife and I

were ministering together at a large family camp. We were using our various gifts effectively—serving, loving, socializing, and all-around working hard. We blended into the routine inconspicuously but with expectations of being productive without the need for shepherding. We both noticed and started to joke about the change in demeanor and fanfare people would shift into whenever our pastor-husbands would come around. We female cardinals were passed by as people were en route to them. They were greeted cheerfully, sought after for conversations and their stories were always laughed at. Some ministry wives are also "flashy" colorful birds like their mates; but I believe many are the lovely, gifted, better camouflaged, and therefore lesser-acknowledged species. This dynamic can be true for any spouse of a highly visible person.

On the one hand it's nice to be the female cardinal; the attention and pressure aren't all on you. You're freer to do your nesting and go about your business unnoticed, with some, but fewer, expectations. However, blending into the bushes can get old too: waiting in line to talk to him at church, doing the "single-parent thing" on Sundays, and going to any public place and waiting while he chats and laughs with parishioners. If your own church is large, it is especially embarrassing when you're greeted in coffee fellowship and asked if you're a first-time visitor. This can be an almost humorous reality to accept and relax in, or it can become a bitter point of jealousy and resentment.

The public side can be painful, but the private side has its own pain as well. Your husband is the need-meeter, taking time to help all the hurting families. He is the good listener, the compassionate, empathetic, wise counselor, and the gifted communicator. He may even be the dream husband other women in the congregation wish they had. You are proud of him, but you find yourself wondering where the dream husband is when he enters his own home. It is his job, his role, his calling to be those things for his flock, but when he comes home to you, he is just an ordinary man. He is exhausted and he needs down time. A man of real integrity is the same intrinsic person at the church or in the home; but in reality, he is just a flawed needy guy like the rest of us. Yet an illusion can exist in our female cardinal brains, that he should be all those wonderful things in an extra special "making up" way to us. We don't want the ordinary man; we want the pastor to pastor us. We want the knight in shining armor to rescue us. We've bought into the fairy tale.

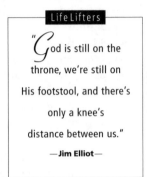

**LifeLifters**

"*G*od is still on the throne, we're still on His footstool, and there's only a knee's distance between us."
—**Jim Elliot**—

This attitude contributes to the bitterness and dissatisfaction many ministry wives feel. It's no wonder 80 percent of ministry wives are unhappy in their role resulting in the exit of so many families from ministry. I've spoken with many wives who feel neglected. They expect his job skills to be his home skills too. They are jealous of the church and almost consider her his mistress. (Granted, some pastors do almost completely neglect their own families. They wrongly prefer the role and the attention to the hard work of intimacy.)

Could it be that we sometimes put all our "eggs" in one basket? Is he really supposed to be husband, pastor, daddy, lover, teacher, and counselor? Are you looking to him to fill your emotional tank instead of being responsible for yourself before God? You may be the only person he can be out of "role" with (his equal, his mutual helpmate, and friend. It is with you he can let his feathers down, be insecure, vulnerable, tired, silly, confused, sad, and relaxed.) He can't be your pastor and your friend and soul mate.

Personally, I'd rather have my husband as my soul mate, and together we can look to our Heavenly Father (the lover of sparrows) for our care.

# chapter ten

# How to Turn Your
# *Prayer Meetings*
# into Blessings

*Jill Briscoe*

Some of the most boring times of my Christian life have been spent in church prayer meetings. Some of the funniest times of my Christian life have been spent in church prayer meetings—and some of the most blessed times. What makes the difference? What ingredients are needed to turn a prayer meeting from a bane into a blessing?

First of all, we have to learn to deal with *Mrs. Mumbler*. Her head is down, and her words are shooting straight into the carpet. All of us are nearly falling off our chairs in an effort to hear.

There is only one way out of this. As the leader of the group, tell everyone (looking straight at Mrs. Mumbler) that we will keep our heads up to pray, speak loud enough for all to hear, and if anyone prays too softly, you will stop the person praying and ask for more volume.

Next, you may have a *Mr. Got-to-tell-you-all-I-know* in the group. This is the one who can't wait to impart scriptural knowledge to the people in the prayer meeting. We trace the journeys of the Children of Israel through the wilderness into the Promised Land; listen to the various prophets (were there really that many?) thunder their exhortations, and finish up with a quick survey of the New Testament theology.

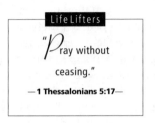

**Life Lifters**

"*P*ray without ceasing."

—**1 Thessalonians 5:17**—

When he eventually stops, everyone is so stunned there is a loud silence, which he mistakes for appreciation!

Then there is *Miss Steal-everything-there-is-to-pray-about-before-you-get-a-turn*. This young lady really *is* a menace. Miss Steal-everything starts. She uses up every item on the prayer list and ends with a triumphant, "So, Lord, continue with us as we pray on." *Little Miss Frightened-out-of-her-mind* is sitting next to her, and of course, is left with absolutely nothing to pray for. She has sat there in horror as item after item was used up, her mind frantically trying to think of some other petition.

Then you have *Mrs. Can't-wait-to-tell-you-all-the-juicy-gossip-I-can't-tell-you-with-my-eyes-open!* This is an obnoxious lady who uses the public prayer meeting to pass on juicy news—all under the disguise of praying for poor so-and-so.

Now this *has* to be stopped. The public prayer meeting was never intended to be a place to reveal private scandals.

Then there is *Mr. Correct-your-prayer-partner.* He is the one who listens to a "starter prayer" and feels it his duty to catch the prayer in midair, sort it out, and deliver it as he knows it was intended to the Almighty!

The leaders should pray about all of these problems, be brave enough to approach the offenders in love and talk with them, and also plan a variety of prayer meetings using different formats to encourage new pray-ers and curtail long ones. A planned format is a helpful way to correct many of these problems.

Not long ago, several of us made a list of the do's and don'ts to be observed in a prayer meeting. Working in pairs, we simply planned a half-hour prayer meeting for our church. The following plan for praying for our church was a result of our committee's work.

## How to Pray for the Church

To inform group members of our class about the needs of the church, we invited several ministry leaders to come and share their needs with the people. Dividing the large group into smaller units, we put a ministry leader with each group for fifteen minutes. For five minutes they prayed about those requests. We had a tremendous response to this. The ministry leaders were delighted, and the group members were thrilled the very next week to hear about the answers to their prayers.

As an example, our maintenance head had been asked to share his problems, and he communicated the need for a student helper to clean the church building in the evenings. They had tried for weeks to find one, but had not been successful. The little group prayed, and the next week the maintenance man returned to ask if he could share the results. *Two* students had applied for the job that very week, and they had employed the one who appeared most suitable!

Here are some other people from your church that you might invite to join you in a prayer time:

Nursery Coordinator
Maintenance Person
Deacon or Elder
Office Personnel
Sunday School Superintendent
Youth Leader
Church Finance Committee Member
Sound System Technician
Tape Ministry Representative
Missions Committee Representative

This is just one of the ideas our group came up with. Maybe you can put some formats together, too. You could collect them, place them in a file, and recruit leaders who would use them in your church prayer meetings. With a little effort and creativity, you can turn your prayer meetings into blessings.

# Author Biographies

**Jill Briscoe** is a popular writer and conference speaker who has authored over forty books. She directs Telling the Truth media ministries with her husband, Stuart, and ministers through speaking engagements around the world. Jill is executive editor of *Just Between Us*, a magazine for ministry wives and women in leadership, and serves on the boards of World Relief and Christianity Today International. Jill and Stuart live in suburban Milwaukee, Wisconsin, and have three grown children and thirteen grandchildren.

**Nancy J. Nordenson** is a freelance writer with a specialty in medical writing. Nancy is the author of the forthcoming book, *Women Who Think*. Married with two sons, she lives in Minneapolis, Minnesota and is a member of the Evangelical Covenant Church denomination.

**Louis McBurney, M.D.** founded Marble Retreat, a counseling center for clergy in the Colorado Rockies, thirty years ago. He and his wife are now looking forward to concentrating on missionary member care and writing. They have three grown children and three grandchildren and live in Marble, Colorado.

**Pamela Binkley** has been involved in Bible Study Fellowship for fifteen years. Studying Scripture is the passion of Pamela's life and watching others grow in spiritual maturity is her greatest joy. Pamela and her husband have been married almost forty years and live in Houston, Texas. She has two grown children.

**Bette Morgan** has been actively involved in organizing and teaching weekly Bible studies and speaking nationally for women's conferences, seminars and retreats for the last thirty years. She is a ministry wife serving alongside her husband, Gerald, who is the director of Church Relations for Mission to the World in Atlanta, Georgia. Currently, she travels with her husband throughout their denomination. Bette is frequently called on as a consultant to local churches for designing, developing, and building a biblical model for women's ministry. Bette has five children and five grandchildren and lives in Suwanee, Georgia.

**Shelly Esser** has been the editor of *Just Between Us*, a magazine for ministry wives and women in leadership, for the last thirteen years. She has written numerous published articles and ministered to women for over twenty years. Her recent book, *My Cup Overflows—A Deeper Study of Psalm 23* encourages women to discover God's shepherd love and care for them. She lives in southeastern Wisconsin, with her husband, John, and four daughters.

**Lydia E. Harris** is a wife, mother, and grandmother who writes articles, devotionals, book reviews, columns, and stories. She has contributed to several books and writes the column, "A Cup of Tea with Lydia" which is published across the United States and Canada. A former teacher, she presents workshops at writers' conferences. Lydia is also involved in a prayer ministry at her church. She and her husband have two grown children and live in Seattle, Washington.

**Elizabeth Greene** has an M.A. in Christian Education and formerly served as a children's ministry pastor for six years at Elmbrook Church in Brookfield, Wisconsin. Elizabeth continues to remain active in children's and women's ministries through teaching and speaking. She lives in Waukesha, Wisconsin, with her husband, Ryan, and two children.

**Ingrid Lawrenz, MSW** is a licensed social worker who has been counseling for seventeen years. Ingrid has been a pastor's wife for twenty-seven years and is currently the senior pastor's wife at Elmbrook Church in suburban Brookfield, Wisconsin. She and her husband, Mel, have two teenagers and live in Waukesha, Wisconsin.

## Dealing with Difficult People

Handling problem
people in your life.
ISBN 0-78143-951-5
ITEM #102350

## Finding God's Will

Embracing God's plan
for your life.
ISBN 0-78143-947-7
ITEM #102346

## Finding Joy

Developing patterns
for a joyful life.
ISBN 0-78143-949-3
ITEM #102348

## Keeping Fresh When You're Frantic

Renewing your spiritual life.
ISBN 0-78143-956-6
ITEM #102355

**Prayer that Works**
Plugging into the
power source.
ISBN 0-78143-953-1
ITEM #102352

**Resolving Conflict**
Stilling the storms of life.
ISBN 0-78143-954-X
ITEM #102353

**The Search for Balance**
Keeping first things first.
ISBN 0-78143-955-8
ITEM #102354

**Spiritual Warfare**
Equipping yourself for battle.
ISBN 0-78143-948-5
ITEM #102347